KAWAII

fruitie cuties!

T0364015

Running Press
Hachette Book Group
1290 Avenue of the Americas, New York, NY 10104
www.runningpress.com
@Running_Press

First Edition: April 2019

Published by Running Press, an imprint of Perseus Books, LLC, a subsidiary of Hachette Book Group, Inc. The Running Press name and logo is a trademark of the Hachette Book Group.

The publisher is not responsible for websites (or their content) that are not owned by the publisher.

ISBN: 978-0-7624-9380-7

contents

INTRODUCTION

Welcome to the happy world of kawaii cross-stitch! Kawaii means "cute" in Japanese, and kawaii style is all about cheerful faces bringing everyday objects to life—like this super-cute fruity bunch.

Kawaii pairs perfectly with cross-stitch—a fun and popular style of embroidery. In cross-stitch, the design is created by making a series of x-shaped stitches on a special fabric called Aida. (There's also a bit of detailing with a technique called backstitch—more on that later!)

This kit contains all the tools you need to stitch three out of the four kawaii fruitie cutie designs. (And if you want to stitch all four, no worries! Cross-stitch fabric and thread can be easily found at your local craft store.) So pick your favorite super-cute kawaii designs—pretty pineapple, blushing berry, mellow melon, or sour lemon—and have fun stitching!

CROSS-STITCH BASICS

Cross-stitch style is a particular style of embroidery, one in which you'll use a relatively blunt needle—called a tapestry needle—to sew *x*-shaped stitches onto your fabric surface, creating a picture (in our case, adorable fruitie cuties). Here are a few basics to get you started!

SUPPLIES

One of the benefits of cross-stitch is how easy it is to get started—you'll only need a few tools to begin working. With cross-stitch fabric, tapestry needles, embroidery floss, a hoop, and some sharp scissors, you'll be whipping up kawaii keepsakes in no time.

fabric

Aida cloth is made specifically for cross-stitch projects. It is comprised of tiny squares so it is easy to see where each stitch in your pattern belongs. There are three pieces of Aida cloth included in this kit to get you started! If you're in need of more or want to do all four patterns provided in the kit, don't fret: Aida is easy to find at your local craft store or online.

needles

For any kind of embroidery project, you'll need a needle to pull your thread through the fabric. With cross-stitch, the best tool is a tapestry needle—the relatively dull point on these needles will go through your fabric without snagging or tearing. There are two needles included in this kit—you only need one while you work, but it doesn't hurt to have an extra on hand.

thread

Thread is the most important, and the most fun, part of your cross-stitch arsenal. All of the patterns in this book use embroidery floss, which is a type of six-strand thread that is especially well-suited to cross-stitch. We've included four skeins of thread that correspond with the patterns in this book.

hoop

The easiest way to keep your fabric nice and taut is to use an embroidery hoop. Included in this kit is a 3-inch plastic hoop; all four patterns in this kit are designed to fit within it. Simply trim the excess cloth or tape it behind the hoop and your masterpiece is ready for display or gifting.

scissors

A pair of regular scissors will do in a pinch, but an extra-sharp pair will come in handy if you need to remove any stitches or get into small areas. Always be careful when using your embroidery scissors.

LET'S GET STITCHIN'

xxxx**X**xxxx

Before you begin stitching your kawaii masterpiece, you'll need to get your fabric ready.

First, you'll need to "load" your fabric onto your hoop: Unscrew the tightening device at the top of your hoop until it is loose enough that you can remove the inner ring. Place your cloth on top of the inner ring so that the ring is centered under your cloth. Then, place the outer hoop over the cloth and the inner hoop, so that you are sandwiching the cloth between the two hoops. Press down so the outer ring covers the inner ring completely, then tighten the screw at the top of the outer hoop so that the fabric is taut.

Next, thread your needle. Find the color that corresponds to the stitches that are in the center of your pattern (more on that in a moment), and cut a piece of thread that is roughly 18 inches long. You'll then want to separate your piece of thread into strands. (Each piece of embroidery floss is made up of six distinct strands, though you will only want to use one at a time when you're stitching these small patterns.) Feed one strand through the eye of your needle, doubling it over so there is an equal amount of thread on either side of the needle and the ends meet. Don't knot the thread.

making
cross-stitches

Your stitches will move from the center of the pattern outward. The patterns in this book use a method called "counted cross-stitch," meaning that you will base your stitches off of a pattern, rather than a design printed on the fabric. With this type of pattern, you'll count the number of stitches in the color you're using and then make those stitches on your fabric. So, to get started, find the center of your fabric—you don't need to be super precise, but try to get as close to the center as possible. This is where you'll want to begin stitching.

Once you've found the center of your fabric, you can begin making stitches.

1 To start, pull your thread up through the small hole at the **bottom left** corner of your starting square, being sure

to leave a one-inch "tail" of floss on the underside of the fabric. Hold on to that tail as you make your next few stitches right on top of it—you'll want the back side of your stitches to cover the tail, securing it in place.

2 Pull the thread up through the fabric and then sew through the **top right** corner of the same square, creating a diagonal stitch. Pull your thread through to the back of the fabric, taking care not to pull it

too tightly—your goal should be a smooth surface, without any puckering from the floss. This is the first half of your stitch.

3 To create the second half of your stitch, sew up from the back of the fabric—through the **bottom right** corner of the square—to the front.

4 Pull your thread relatively taut, and then cross the square diagonally, sewing down through the **top left**

hole. This will create the x shape of your cross-stitch.

5 Continue by making a stitch in the **bottom left** corner of the square next to your completed stitch. This square borders your first stitch, and shares two holes with it.

finishing touches

The smile details are made using a technique called backstitch. To begin, thread your needle with black floss and weave it into a few stitches on the back of your work. This will secure it.

Following the pattern for placement, bring the needle up to the surface and make a stitch over (or across, depending on the pattern) one square of Aida. To make the next stitch, come up one square away from the previous stitch and go back down into the previous stitch. (Hence, *back*stitch!)

helpful tips

✖ For a polished look, make all your stitches in the same direction and order: from the bottom left to the top right, and then the bottom right to the top left.

✖ To display your work, soak it in a warm bath to remove any hoop creases. Let dry flat. (Do not wring.)

fruitie cuties

PATTERNS

PRETTY PINEAPPLE

thread colors

- ✖ Color 1
- ✖ Color 2
- ✖ Color 3
- ✖ Color 4

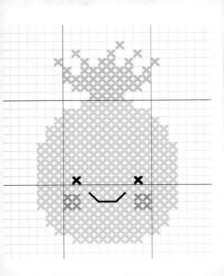

BLUSHING BERRY

thread colors

- ✖ Color 1
- ✖ Color 2
- ✖ Color 3
- ✖ Color 4

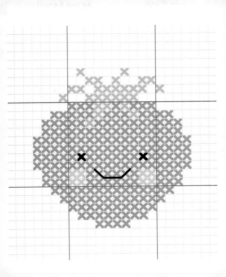

MELLOW MELON

thread colors

- ✖ Color 1
- ✖ Color 2
- ✖ Color 3
- ✖ Color 4

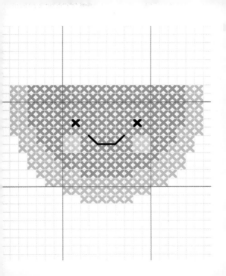

SOUR LEMON

thread colors

- ✖ Color 1
- ✖ Color 2
- ✖ Color 3

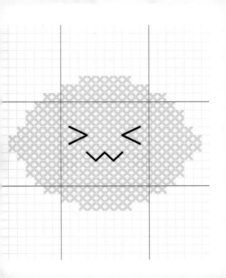

This book has been bound using handcraft methods and Smyth-sewn to ensure durability.

The box and interior were designed by Susan Van Horn.

The introduction and text on page 22 were written by Sosae and Dennis Caetano.

The illustrations and patterns were created and illustrated by Sosae and Dennis Caetano.